U

C000058902

unofficial and unauthorised

EDITED BY **JUSTYN BARNES**

CARLTON
BOOKS

This edition published in 2008

First published in 2001

Copyright © 2001 Manchester United Plc
Text and design copyright © 2001, 2004, 2006 Carlton Books Ltd

Manufactured and distributed by
Carlton Books Limited
20 Mortimer Street
London W1T 3JW

A CIP catalogue record for this book is available
from the British Library

ISBN: 978-1-84442-078-0

Project Editor: Martin Corteel
Project Art Director: Darren Jordan
Production: Sarah Corteel

Printed in China

Football, as someone said, is all about opinions. And one club generates more opinions than most. Whether it's in the media, the dressing room or down the pub, Manchester United is frequently the topic of conversation. Hardly surprising really, when you consider that many of the game's most dramatic events, finest players and greatest matches have United at their core.

So here's a collection of some of the best soundbites, from the inspired to the insane, the profound to the surreal. Whether you're after eyewitness accounts, expert punditry or insider anecdotes, you should find it here. Together with praise, jealousy, warmth and regret for the most famous football club in the world. Let's face it, everybody's talking about them.

' For men who work on the shop floor, the one highlight of their week is to go and watch football. Matt Busby used to say you should give that man something he can't do himself, something exciting. That's why Manchester United always play attacking football. '

Sir Bobby Charlton

‘ I had always had a feeling that one day I would join United. I don't know whether it was wishful thinking or just a sixth sense about my destiny. ’

Denis Law

‘ I'm in love with Manchester United.
It is like finding a wife who has given
me the perfect marriage. ’

Eric Cantona

❛ I think they've got problems. You just can't win anything with kids. **❜**

Match Of The Day *pundit* **Alan Hansen**'s *verdict after a young United team lost 1–3 to Aston Villa on the first day of the 1995–96 season, but the 'kids' went on to win the League and FA Cup double*

‘ When you look down the list of who you are going to get points off, you mark Manchester United down as zero. ’

Derby County manager **Jim Smith**

'I don't look at Manchester United. They've got 70,000 gates, they've got the Beckhams and so on, all young and hungry. My dream is to become second best – only then will I start worrying about the freaks from across the Pennines!'

Leeds United manager **David O'Leary**

❝ You have to give Fergie credit. He has brought United on leaps and bounds... the bastard! **❞**

Liverpool manager **Roy Evans** *(February 1998)*

❛ Sir Matt Busby came into the dressing room after we'd become champions. He said very little but his expression said it all. His beloved Manchester United were back on top. ❜

Bryan Robson *on the end of the 26-year wait for League Championship victory*

'The afternoon of 2 May 1993, when we were crowned the champions of England was the day I truly became the manager of Manchester United. Until that fancy bit of silverware was in our grasp, nothing could be taken for granted. '

Sir Alex Ferguson

❛ The players that I respect are the ones sitting next to me in the dressing room. ❜

Roy Keane

‘ When we meet up with England I get envious when I see what David Beckham, Paul Scholes and the Neville brothers have won. They have achieved more than us and I'd be lying if I said I'm not jealous. ’

Liverpool striker **Robbie Fowler**

' I can name three or four players off the top of my head who try to wind me up. If a player's going to try and do it, I can tell in the first minute. **"**

Roy Keane

' I've had a few clashes with Dennis Wise over the years, but it's nothing personal. Once you are off the football pitch, it's all over and done with. '

Nicky Butt

' Nicky Butt's a real Manchester boy. A bit of a scallywag. He comes from Gorton where it is said they take the pavements in of a night time. '

Sir Alex Ferguson

'I was a bad boy at school. I once got in trouble for setting a science lab on fire. We were messing around with the gas taps and set some magnesium in a test-tube alight and a fire started. But we didn't do it on purpose... honest!'

Nicky Butt

' I got the cane once for throwing a snowball in class. My hands were still cold when the teacher hit me and it was very sore! **'**

Teddy Sheringham

❝ When we went paintballing, it turned into a bit of a free-for-all. It hurts when you get hit and there's a few sadistic people in our squad – David May springs to mind. ❞

Gary Neville

‘If he's got a temperament, wait until he sees my temperament.’

Alex Ferguson *wasn't frightened of Eric Cantona's reputation when he signed him in November 1992*

‘ Perhaps I should be an example to people, but I do not think that way, I do not react that way. I am simply me. ’

Eric Cantona

' Apparently when you head a football, you lose brain cells, but it doesn't bother me... I'm a horse. No-one's proved it yet have they? **'**

*United central defender **David May**
has headed a lot of balls*

❝ I don't know about making referees professional. They love themselves enough as it is now. **❞**

Paul Scholes

' David Beckham and I were standing in the centre-circle when the crowd started calling me names. I said to him, 'I suppose you're used to all this.' He grinned and replied, 'Yeah, but in my case, it's not true!' '

Referee **Graham Poll**

❝ My Nan loves to watch me on TV, but is always remarking on how often I seem to argue with referees. Worse than that my Nan is an excellent lip-reader! ❞

David Beckham *(May 1998)*

'I find it amusing that Roy Keane has this really hard image. Once you get to know him, he's not as bad as he's portrayed. I like to chat with him. He is what he is and I like that.'

Dwight Yorke

❮ Roy Keane is Damien, the devil incarnate off the film *The Omen*. He's evil. Even in training. ❯

Ryan Giggs

❮ I'm moody and grumpy most of the time. ❯

Roy Keane

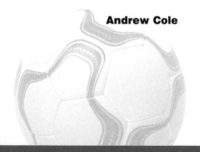

'Nothing depresses me. I just get on with things. Life's too short.'

Andrew Cole

‘ If you are going to break your leg, do it at United. I received total support and the lads couldn't have been better. ’

Dion Dublin *who went on to play for England*

‘ If I thought personal glory
was more important than team
glory, I would have taken up
an individual sport. ’

Eric Cantona

‘Some of the players call me
‘Gaffer’... and when Gary Pallister
wants to take a weekend off,
he calls me ‘God’!’

Alex Ferguson *(December 1995)*

‘ For the first year I was a pro, when the manager walked into the room I just shut up and sat up as if I was at school. If I heard him coming down the stairs, I would turn around and go back into the dressing room. I was definitely scared of him. ’

Phil Neville *on Sir Alex Ferguson*

' People don't see him when he comes in and pinches our chocolates, or when he sings to us! The manager thinks he's got an excellent singing voice and well... we always agree with the manager. '

Lyn Laffin, *Sir Alex's P.A., relates another side to the Gaffer's character*

'I've sung every song in the world in the bath. I'm thinking of releasing a CD called 'Singalong with Fergie!''

Sir Alex 'Pavarotti' Ferguson

'For a Welshman, I can't sing.'

Ryan Giggs

❛ My dad does know Romeo from the group and he's played in a few bands with him. But my dad was definitely not the drummer in Showaddywaddy. ❜

Former United striker **Dion Dublin**
denies a scurrilous rumour

'I'm amazed that someone with hands the size of shovels can play anything from boogie-woogie to Bach on the piano.'

Former United goalkeeping coach **Alan Hodgkinson** *admired Peter Schmeichel's musical skills*

‘It wasn't my choice to become a goalkeeper, but I was probably too violent to play outfield. ’

Peter Schmeichel

❛My first goal for United for the youth team against Preston at the Cliff training ground. A free-kick from 25 yards believe it or not... Honestly! Becks was in the team, but he wasn't taking them back then.❜

Gary Neville

‘I find it natural to score goals. When I head towards goal, I know exactly what to do.’

Ole Gunnar Solskjaer, *then an almost unknown Norwegian striker, speaking soon after he signed for United in 1996 – he wasn't exaggerating*

' Coley calls me jigsaw because I fall to pieces in front of goal. '

Phil Neville

I don't think Phil ever scores a goal to be honest. He scored one once in the under-11s! At school he was renowned for scoring own goals!

Gary Neville *on his brother's goalscoring prowess*

‘ I can't believe it, I actually scored! My first goal in 90 League and cup games! Strangely, Ole Gunnar Solskjaer had a premonition I was going to do it. He came up to me three times in the hour before kick-off and said, 'You're going to score today, Phil. Remember what I say.' I just laughed. ’

Phil Neville *on his winning goal against Chelsea on 28 February 1998*

❝ I was never fined for the Sharpey Shuffle, but the Boss threatened to. I said if he stopped me doing it I would stop scoring goals! ❞

Lee Sharpe's *unique goal celebrations didn't impress Alex Ferguson*

❛ Well, I rose like a salmon at the far post, but Pally rose like a fresher salmon and towered above me, headed the ball at the keeper, the keeper fumbled, then I saw a sudden flash of brilliant red and leathered it into the roof of the net with my left foot sponsored by Diadora boots. ❜

David May's vivid description of his goal in United's 4–0 thrashing of Porto in March 1997

‘ It got to the point where I just thought, 'I'm going to take everyone on.' And when I got through I just hit it as hard as I could. David Seaman got a lot of stick, but it really was the only place I could have put it to beat him. ’

Ryan Giggs *describing his wonder goal in the 1999 FA Cup semi-final replay against Arsenal*

' Ryan's goal was meant to be. A higher power was at work. **'**

Arsenal defender **Tony Adams**

' Ryan just put his head down, ran like he always does, didn't pass and got lucky. **'**

Nicky Butt*'s view of Giggs' goal*

❛ Racism is an abomination. I don't understand why people are afraid of different races coming together. When races come together cultures are enriched. ❜

Eric Cantona

❛ I'm proud of my black background. Half of my family is black. Because of the way I look, people don't realise it. It really doesn't bother me that people automatically assume I'm white. The people who are close to me, and care about me, know and that is all that matters. **❜**

Ryan Giggs

❛ Even today when I see archive films of Duncan Edwards it really upsets me. We'll never get over Munich. The mood in the city was ghastly... The whole country felt for the club. Even in the 1958 Cup Final, everyone was on Manchester United's side... a bit different from today ❜

Norman Williams, *United supporter*

❛ We used to go here, there and everywhere in groups, loads of us. We went to Butlins together, as a youth side we had our first trip abroad to Switzerland together. We were pals, best pals... and then the crash happened. ❜

'Busby Babe' **Wilf McGuiness** *who missed the fateful trip to Red Star Belgrade through injury*

‘ I can still remember the first television pictures. Snow falling in the darkness, the flakes illuminated by camera lighting and the sudden burst of flashbulbs. Snow, twisted metal, seats which had been hurled from the aircraft, overcoats and odd shoes. ’

Tom Tyrrell *sportswriter and United fan*

' I was having a shave in the kitchen when my wife shouted out from the front room, 'Have you heard the news?' I'd shaved half of my face, but I don't think I shaved the other half for three days. I was absolutely devastated. '

Harold Wood *Club steward*

‘ It may seem odd but when I think of Manchester United I think of Roger Byrne, Duncan Edwards and Eddie Colman before the Munich aircrash, and of Harry Gregg, Bill Foulkes and Nobby Stiles afterwards. Best, Law and Crerand were replaceable somehow. They weren't the heart of the team. ’

Sir Bobby Charlton

❝ The intense pride in their city has made a deep impression on me and I now regard myself as an adopted Mancunian. **❞**

Sir Alex Ferguson *on being awarded the Freedom of the City of Manchester*

'When I was about eight, I tossed a coin with my best friend and said: 'Heads we go to Old Trafford, tails we go to Maine Road.' The rest is history. '

Robert Powell *actor and United fan*

❝ I saw the United team at the airport once. I was just double star-struck, man. **❞**

Shaun Ryder
Happy Mondays vocalist and United fan

❛ My wife told me that I loved Manchester United more than her. I told her that I loved Manchester City more than her... ❜

An unnamed **member of the Carrickfergus Branch of the Supporters' Club** *explains why his marriage ended in divorce*

‘ Matt Busby liked a joke. Could he tell a joke? Could he hell! He'd get the punchline half-right and I'd say what it should have been. He'd reply, 'That's what I meant' and I'd roar. ’

Jimmy Tarbuck

‘He treated my Dad with a lot of respect and always took time out for him. I mean, little things are important to us and Matt even remembered what sort of sandwiches my Dad liked.’

George Best

‘ We had a few problems with the wee fella, but I prefer to remember his genius. ’

Sir Matt Busby *on George Best*

❛George Best has ice in his veins, warmth in his heart and timing and balance in his feet.❜

Danny Blanchflower

' When I was eighteen, nineteen,
I went down to join the Welsh
squad a couple of times with a
bit of a beard. They started
calling me 'George' from then
on, and the name's stuck! '

Ryan Giggs

" I couldn't tell you which hotel we stayed at, whether we had a post-match banquet... it's just a blank. But the game itself, I can remember almost every kick. I was fortunate enough to score in the Final. I remember the ball being cleared and coming to me. And I knew I was going to score, I just knew. "

George Best *on the 1968 European Cup Final victory*

❝ It was an unbelievable night. I watched football as a kid and saw players go up to the Royal Box at Wembley and thought, 'What are they crying for?' But as soon as the final whistle went, I just sunk to my knees. I couldn't stop myself. ❞

Ryan Giggs
on the 1999 European Champions League Final win

❝ The last time I saw a person dance on a table was Giggsy after we won the European Cup. He fell off and everyone was a bit worried, but he just got straight back on the table and carried on! ❞

Teddy Sheringham

❝I'm not one for falling over easily. I'm not one for diving in the penalty box. I don't think the team has ever got any penalties from me.❞

United's very honest striker **Andrew Cole**

❝ Rumours escalate in football. With me it went from, 'I don't know if his ankle is right' to 'He's running round on a stump!' It's a game of Chinese Whispers. ❞

Paul Parker's football career suffered a severe downturn after leaving Old Trafford

' There is nothing more stupid than a footballer who pretends to be more indispensable than the ball. Rather than run with the ball, make the ball do the work, give it and look quickly. Look around quickly and you will be the best. '

Advice from **Cantona senior** *to a young Eric*

Caller: "I'd just want to know – how many times does a full back have to make an overlapping run before you see him?"

David Beckham: "If it was a different full back, he'd get the ball!"

Gary Neville *uses an MUTV phone-in with David Beckham to make a point*

' If I had to pick a weakness in Beckham's game it's his left foot. But that's like saying Maradona's right foot wasn't too clever. '

George Best

'My wife's always saying, 'Why don't you grow up?' and I say, 'Why should I? I'm enjoying myself being silly and young!''

Sir Alex Ferguson

‘ You need to get the balance right. You have to take it seriously because it's your job and you're paid to win things, but you should enjoy each moment because there will come a time when you won't be able to play football again. ’

Dwight Yorke

‘There's quite a few funny sights in the dressing room, but the thing that makes me happiest is Yorkie's smile. It makes everyone else smile too!’

Ole Gunnar Solskjaer *on the ray of sunshine that is his fellow striker Dwight Yorke*

'In the changing room, Keaney would say, 'Watch this,' and he'd start humming or singing a song near Gary Pallister. Five minutes later, Pally would be singing the same song. It never failed, that one.'

Ryan Giggs

‘ My wife named our goldfish 'Caster' after the character played by Nicolas Cage played in the film *Face Off*. It's a small fish with black fins... Cage wears this black coat and when it's blowing in the wind, he looks like our goldfish. ’

Jaap Stam

‘ We've always had dogs in our family. Where I come from in Cork they think there's something wrong with you if you don't. The first one was a real old mongrel off the streets. I think his name was 'Lucky'... lucky to find us. ’

Dog-loving **Roy Keane**

'Fabien Barthez is a fantastic character. Once he came into the office and told me he needed a woman to take care of him. What he really meant was that he needed a housekeeper! '

Lyn Laffin, *Sir Alex's P.A., also looks after the players*

‘ We all make an extra effort for the foreign players to make them feel comfortable… Having said that, if they're not working hard enough they get shouted at! ’

Roy Keane

‘ It's a panic buy. **’**

Former Liverpool captain **Emlyn Hughes**
when United bought Eric Cantona

'Eric Cantona is the best prepared footballer I've ever had. He's first at the training ground, he does his own warm-up and then he does ours. He trains brilliantly and then he practices after training and he's the last to leave the car park, signing autographs. He's happy to do hospital visits whenever you ask him to do anything. He's a model pro, an absolute dream footballer.'

Alex Ferguson

' It's not a case of signing autographs so that people will think I'm a nice guy, but rather that I don't want them to have a bad experience. I don't want to hurt them by letting them down. '

Eric Cantona

‘ When you see Eric Cantona brushing up his skills, you know that no-one can be satisfied with their standard. ’

Ryan Giggs

'Eric Cantona is a great player,
but he is not as good as
Ryan Giggs.'

Johann Cruyff

' Ryan Giggs is the detonator, the man who can make Manchester United explode. '

Jean Tigana

‘The manager doesn't want me to live like a monk. If he tried to make me live like a monk my football would go down the drain. He understands that, we've had that conversation.’

Ladies' man **Dwight Yorke**

❛ I don't really like the attention from girls – apart from anything else I already have a girlfriend. I like supporters of football whatever sex they are, but it's not so great when you're on a night-out and girls just sit next to you... but to be honest it doesn't happen to me that often anyway. ❜

Gary Neville *(October 1996)*

‘I chose Eric Cantona because
I'm impressed by his sincerity,
sensitivity and his genuineness.
He is a passionate, larger
than life person who
symbolises youth!’

Designer **Paco Rabanne** *on why he chose Eric to
model his clothes at a fashion show in 1993*

‘I think I'd like to be in the fashion industry. I don't really know anything about it, but I reckon I'm great at choosing clothes. The things I buy are the best clothes in the world – or at least that's what I think.’

Paul Parker

‘ My Dad tells me that I've always wanted to play here. He said when I first saw Old Trafford I just stood and stared for an hour. ’

Gary Neville

‘ I'd seen Manchester United on TV, but when I went to Old Trafford it was, 'Am I really in Manchester?' I didn't watch the game, I was just looking at all the people. ’

Hilda Fortune, *mother of United winger Quinton Fortune, recalls her first visit to Old Trafford*

'They should have brought in the ten-yard rule years ago. If Schmeichel was in goal and the ball was moved forward because one of his defenders was arguing with the referee, he'd have come out and smacked them because his goal's at threat.'

Gordon Strachan

'I was only ever punished once by my parents when I was very young and stole a newspaper from a shop. I was probably too young to read it and I don't know why I did it. I was kept in my room for a full week. It was like a prison. But I never stole again.'

Peter Schmeichel

‘ You could knock the worst pass ever to Sparky and he would rip people's necks off to get it. At the time he wouldn't make gestures to make you look stupid, but a while later he'd come up to you and say, 'If you give me another pass like that, I'll have yer!' ’

Paul Parker *on the "best all-round footballer I played with" – Mark Hughes*

' I found it very difficult returning to Old Trafford for the first time. I got a marvellous reception, but the game just passed me by. Some of the Chelsea lads had a go at me after we scored. They reckoned I didn't jump up and down enough. '

Mark Hughes

❛Managing this club can become an obsession.❜

Sir Alex Ferguson

'I remember Viv Anderson saying to me once: 'You're off your head being a manager. I wouldn't be a manager in a million years.' When he took the Barnsley job in 1993, his first phone call was from me. I said: 'Welcome to the madhouse!''

Sir Alex Ferguson

‘ You shouldn't be nuts, but it doesn't matter if you are a bit peculiar. ’

Peter Schmeichel
identifies the essential quality of a goalkeeper

‘ Peter Schmeichel once asked for a shoe horn. Schmikes keeps you on your toes every match. It can take 20 minutes just to set out his stuff. He doesn't always require the shoe horn, but I keep it handy just in case. ’

Norman Davies *retired Manchester United kitman*

❛Teddy Sheringham did all the hard work for me and I just managed to get a toe on the ball to steer it in. I have never had a better feeling than that and I doubt I ever will. It'll take a couple of years to sink in.❜

Ole Gunnar Solskjaer *on scoring the winning goal in the 1999 European Champions League Final*

‘ Even though it was the last minute, I was quite calm. I just knew we'd score, I really did. And as soon as we equalised I knew that there was only one team that could win it. I could see that Munich were gone ’

*Suspended captain **Roy Keane**'s view from the bench*

‘ It makes me cringe just thinking about it. To this day, I have never watched a video of that game. ’

Jim Leighton *remembers his calamitous performance in the 1990 FA Cup Final, when United drew 3–3 with Crystal Palace and he was replaced by Les Sealey in the replay which United won 1–0*

'The lads used to call me 'the Judge' because I sat on the bench so much.'

Les Sealey

❝ I'm sure Arsenal fans are working on some new chants, but they can sing what they like. I've got three nice medals to show them. **❞**

Ex-Spurs striker **Teddy Sheringham** *looks forward to his next match against Arsenal in summer 1999 soon after winning the Treble*

❛ Over the years people called several players the new Duncan Edwards... first Dave Mackay, then Bryan Robson. But none of them came close. He was the only player who ever made me feel inferior. **❜**

Sir Bobby Charlton

❛Everybody now talks about Cantona being the main catalyst of United's latter-day glories. But without Bryan Robson, I maintain United might not have had the same stature when Eric arrived. Robson was the essence of United.❜

Ron Atkinson

‘ Robbo was coming to the end of his career when I joined United, but I still got a sense of how important he was at the club. He was a top player and just to play with him towards the end of his career was an honour. ’

Roy Keane *on legendary midfielder Bryan Robson*

‘ In my playing days, you had confrontations but the whole team didn't pile in with their handbags. I think football's become a game of prima donnas. I like watching rugby where players get stuck into each other, but they just get up and get on with it. ’

George Best *bemoans modern players' behaviour*

‘ Even when we played Leyton Orient away, there were 18,000 in the ground and more locked out. The crowds at home were great, but we really noticed it away because each game was a sell-out. That gave us a boost. It made us feel everyone was pulling together. ’

Sammy McIlroy *on fans' support in the 1974–75 season when United were promoted from Division Two*

‟ I love pleasing United fans, but I also get a kick out of being on the pitch and having the power to aggravate thousands of opposing fans without them being able to do anything about it. ”

Mark Hughes

‘I want people to clap me, I want people to like me, I don't want to be booed all the time.**’**

David Beckham

❛ After the 1994 FA Cup Final, I just sank to the floor and all my emotions poured out. There were tears, I cried. But there's nothing wrong with that. ❜

Peter Schmeichel *remembers United's 1994 Double triumph*

❝ When I went down on my knees I strained my ligaments and I was out for the whole summer. ❞

Ole Gunnar Solskjaer *reveals the cost of his European Champions League Final-winning goal celebrations*

❛If I were to go away on a promotional trip and I had to choose one team-mate to go with me, it'd be Ole. I like the way he thinks and how he expressed himself. He'd be good company.❜

Teddy Sheringham

❝ If I were to play a character in a film, it would be the hero played by Antonio Banderas in *Desperado*. In normal life, I try and behave as my parents brought me up to, so it'd be nice to escape their upbringing for a while. ❞

Ole Gunnar Solskjaer

‘ We can play badly, we can defend badly, we can shoot badly, but the one thing that always remains intact is the team spirit. ’

Gary Neville

❝ Other teams have better individual players but nobody has a better team than Manchester United. ❞

*Sturm Graz coach **Ivica Osim** after his team had been outclassed for the fourth time in a row at Old Trafford in March 2001*

' We had fights, and I mean punch-ups, every day. But it didn't matter. We were men enough to take it and forget about it come kick-off time. It didn't matter whether Nobby had chinned Denis or Denis had chinned Bill Foulkes, we were all aiming for the same thing ultimately... '

George Best

❛ ... and by matchday, you had
to be friends because there was
only one bath! **❜**

George Best

‘You go to any factory or office and not everyone is going to like each other. Of course, you are going to have clashes. It's not say we won't have a good do at Christmas and come Saturday, we will all want to win and we will help each other out.’

Roy Keane

‘ I never socialised with Eric. My wife and I always said we would have him over, but we never got round to it. We always called round for the rent, but never to ask him over. That's terrible really, isn't it? ’

Eric Cantona's former team-mate and landlord
Mark Hughes

❛ As YTS players, we were all assigned to clean someone's boots. I got Eric Cantona which I was well pleased with... although Brian McClair was the biggest tipper! **❜**

Wes Brown

❛I play with a certain passion and fire. I have to accept that sometimes this fire does harm.❜

Eric Cantona, *before the infamous kung-fu incident at Selhurst Park in January 1995*

❛ I don't think any player in the
history of football will get the
sentence he got – unless they
had killed Bert Millichip's dog. **❜**

Alex Ferguson *slams Eric's nine-month ban*
(Millichip was Football Association Chairman at the time)

❝ When the seagulls follow the trawler, it is because they think sardines will be thrown into the sea. Merci. ❞

Eric Cantona's enigmatic utterance after his court case in March 1995

❛The seagulls following the boat represent Cantona's fans and the press who are always pursuing him. The trawler is a symbol of the judicial system which almost incarcerated him. The sardines represent Cantona himself, and the other players, who feel they are products in the capitalist system and world of sport.❜

French literature professor **Rufus Doisneau** *offers an explanation*

❛My lawyer wanted me to talk. I could have said, 'The curtains are pink but I love them.'❜

Eric Cantona *offers an alternative explanation*

❝ You couldn't have asked much more of a man who was under the most intense pressure, but he appeared about as relaxed as someone wandering down to the local shops for a pint of milk. ❞

Alan Hansen *on Eric's comeback game against Liverpool on 1 October 1995*

' It got the team spirit going, that's for sure. He's come back from what I thought was a very severe punishment. Some fans go a bit far and I think a lot of players would like to do what Eric did. There's been a lot said about the bloke in the stand that night and, fair enough, maybe he didn't deserve a size 12 boot in the throat, but some fans are really bad. Anyway, Eric got his punishment, did his time and that's the end of it. '

Roy Keane *(December 1996)*

' A survey was conducted of the world's female population asking them if they would sleep with Bill Clinton. 80 percent of them answered, 'What, again?' '

Peter Schmeichel *tells a joke (April 1998)*

Interviewer: "What do you say to the rumour that Gary Neville has been stealing bodies from graveyards and building some kind of creature from the parts in his garage?"

Denis Irwin: "I don't think it's Nev. He's just lays up in his house all day. If you'd said any other player then maybe..."

*A spoof interviewer from the **Mick Molloy Show** livens up a press call in Australia in summer 1999*

‘ Liz Hurley, she's nice. I'd take her to Pizza Express – no posh restaurants. We'd go for a pizza then to watch *Grease* or something. ’

Phil Neville *describes his dream date*
(December 1996)

' Normally, Becks never wears socks on matchdays, but apparently he had some on yesterday and I am reliably informed that they were adorned with images of a popular girl band. Girl gets expensive necklace, boy gets socks. Isn't it always the case? '

Brian McClair *(February 1998)*

‘Football is what brought me here to Manchester United. But God put me on earth, He created everything. If He takes football away from me, I've still got God. And if football stays with me I've still got God.’

Quinton Fortune's response to Bill Shankly's famous *"Football is more important than life and death" comment*

❛ Certainly take the advice of others
but always, always be yourself. **❜**

Eric Cantona

❝We had results e-mailed to us.
Knowing that the League was
going on was great for team
morale – it whiles away the hours
when you're sitting in your tent
freezing cold!❞

Neil Williams, *an Arctic explorer
who wore his United shirt at the North Pole, explains how
United's 1996 Double success helped him get there*

' He's very bossy. Like, he'll say, 'Go and get this,' or, 'Go and get that.' Because he's the older brother, he has the remote control and if he orders room service I'm the one who has to get up and open the door. '

Phil Neville *described what it's like to share a room with Gary on away trips*

'The six of us have all grown up together. It would be strange if one left the club. Say Gary Neville left, it'd be strange... but it would be a lot quieter.'

Ryan Giggs

❛Describing my performance, *The Guardian* reporter wrote: 'Gary Neville spent the first half striking attitudes reminiscent of those confronted by papier maché aliens in *The Outer Limits*.' I think it means I got roasted by Wanchope!❜

Gary Neville *offers a succinct verdict on his performance at Derby in October 1997*

'Being dropped is the sort of thing that spurs me on... If I'd just let it happen and said, 'Well, okay', I wouldn't have got any further than my first ten games in a Millwall shirt.'

Teddy Sheringham

❛ I like to think I've handled my fame well. There aren't too many things I look back on and think, 'Oh, I wish I hadn't done that.' I don't have many regrets. ❜

Ryan Giggs

' Who am I more scared of – the gaffer or my missus? Neither. Always have your alibi ready – that's my motto! **'**

Roy Keane

‘In Turin, Gentile was marking me and I remember trying to get a cross in and he just stood on my shin. Later on, I was waiting for a corner and Gentile pulled a hair from under my armpit. I'd never had that before.’

Former United winger **Steve Coppell** *recalls his painful lesson in the Italian art of defending during United's 1978 UEFA Cup tie against Juventus*

' When I do quit football, it'll be at the top. I certainly wouldn't contemplate playing for teams that are any less successful than Manchester United or playing for the reserves. Once I feel I'm not at the top any more, I'll quit. '

Eric Cantona *talking in the summer of 1996, a year before he retired*

❛In 30 or 40 years time, I'll probably boast about having played with Eric… Even before I came to the club I looked up to him and admired his skills. And I admire him even more now after I've trained with him and got to know him as a person. He was a huge influence at the club and gave everybody a lift with his presence. That is probably what I'll miss most of all.❜

Ole Gunnar Solskjaer
on hearing of Eric's retirement

'When we won the Premiership in 1999, Dwight Yorke lifted the trophy and the crown fell off. I was in the crowd and turned to a total stranger and said: 'Great! I'll have to get that fixed on Monday!' She looked at me as though I was a total madman.'

Manchester United Museum curator **Mark Wylie**

‘ I think the fans appreciate my attitude, and I'd like to think there's no crap about me. What you see is what you get. ’

Roy Keane

‘It's not my fault I never seem to win attacking headers... I need some decent crosses!’

Jaap Stam *on his lack of goals –*
David Beckham and Ryan Giggs might not agree

❛We all agree, Jaap Stam is harder than Arnie!❜

United fans' *chant at Sturm Graz's Arnold Schwarzenegger Stadium (December 2000)*

' Paul Scholes is probably the most complete player at United. He is the type of player I like, someone with special abilities. I wouldn't know who to compare him with. '

Scholes' former team-mate **Jordi Cruyff**

❛ I can recognise the way I move but it's a much better player than me. It can do backheels and stuff like that. ❜

Paul Scholes *admires the cyber-Scholesy created for a computer game*

❝Nobody's going to tell me I'm the world's best, but no-one's going to tell me I'm a crap footballer either. I have belief in myself, simple as that.❞

Teddy Sheringham

‘ Teddy has always been a thinking man's player, like Franz Beckenbauer and Bobby Moore. ’

George Best

A lot of the lads here have nice cars, but they're young and they're single and you can't take the money with you. I've never seen a coffin with pockets.

Roy Keane

❝ If, as some people think, there is such a thing as reincarnation, I'd love to come back as an eagle. I love the way eagles move, the way they soar, the way they gaze. ❞

Eric Cantona

❝ United haven't done anything
special this season. ❞

Arsene Wenger *the week before United
beat Arsenal 6–1 in the 2000–01 Premiership*

❝This team never loses. They just
run out of time.**❞**

United coach **Steve McClaren**

❛ If anything the hunger is getting stronger and stronger. ❜

Roy Keane

❛ Roy Keane can become a manager because he is a natural born leader. You've either got it or you haven't and leadership qualities definitely stand out in Roy. I respect him a lot. **❜**

Laurent Blanc

‘D.I.E.G.O., D.I.E.G.O. …’

*United fans rework the Ottowan dance classic 'D.I.S.C.O.' in
tribute to new Red cult hero* **Diego Forlan**

' The fans were singing my song for ages and I was like, 'Oh my God!' The buzz it gave me was incredible. **'**

Young star **John O'Shea** *enjoys a crowd rendition of 'When Johnny goes marching down the wing, O'Shea, O'Shea'.*

❛ My goal for this year is to become
the complete striker. **❜**

Ruud van Nistelrooy's *undemanding 2003 New
Year's resolution!*

'The variety of Van Nistelrooy's goals is incredible. If a cross comes in you know he'll be on the end of it, but he's also capable of picking the ball up 40 yards out and scoring. Phenomenal.'

George Best

❛ I feel really sad about leaving but I have to move on. I've always been a United fan and will always follow the team. ❜

David Beckham, *June 2003*

‘ I've known David since he was 11 and it's been a pleasure to see him grow and develop into the player he has become. I wish him and his family every success in the future and thank him for his service to the club. ’

Sir Alex Ferguson

‘ David is a good friend, but it's no different to when Eric Cantona or Bryan Robson left. Manchester United will move on, as we have in the past. Inside the club, we have already moved on. ’

Phil Neville *on life after Becks, July 2003*

' Bigger players than David have left in the past and will leave in the future. But the spirit will stay in the team because we still have a big group of players here who remain the heartbeat of the team. '

Nicky Butt

❝ When I was little I followed Manchester United and because my name is Eric, everyone used to call me Cantona. When I was watching United games on TV I would copy him by wearing my collars up! ❞

Eric Djemba Djemba *on growing up in Cameroon*

❛I'm from France so of course I like the sun. But if you are playing for Manchester United you don't care about the weather!❜

David Bellion

' Anyone who knows me will tell you I'm not flash. I'm just a normal kind of guy who happens to play football. I think fans can see if people are flash and we haven't got one flash person in our squad. '

Rio Ferdinand

' You look around the Nike HQ and see people like Michael Jordan and Tiger Woods have buildings named after them. That's what I want – Ferdinand Towers in my honour! I want to join the legends. '

Rio Ferdinand

❝ This club has always had players who show their true colours when the going gets tough dating back to the era of Nobby Stiles, Paddy Crerand and Bobby Charlton through to players like Bryan Robson, Mark Hughes, Steve Bruce and on to today's crop of monsters! That is why Manchester United have had so much success. ❞

Sir Alex Ferguson *reflects on United's amazing 2002-03 Premiership title triumph*

❝ For pure ability and talent, player for player, this is the best United team I've played in. And it can get better. We are champions now and that gives you an extra bit of confidence. **❞**

Ryan Giggs *looks ahead after winning his eighth Premiership winners' medal*

' When I knew about the bid from United there was only one place I was going to go. The players here are unbelievable, the club has fans all over the world and hopefully I can do well. '

Wayne Rooney *joins for £27 million in summer 2004*

' Rooney can be the best in the world at 25 if he knows you need to train hard, go to bed early and be careful what you eat. **'**

Eric Cantona

‘Unfortunately it was a very bad bottle of wine and he was complaining, so when we go to Old Trafford for the second leg, on my birthday, I will take a beautiful bottle of Portuguese wine.’

Jose Mourinho *on his post-match tipple with Sir Alex*

❝ It has been a great honour and privilege for me to play for Manchester United for over 12 years... in front of the best supporters in the world. ❞

Roy Keane *says goodbye.*

❝ The fans will be upset because they loved him. He was a great leader. The best thing about Roy Keane is that you knew where you stood with him. **❞**

David Beckham *on Roy Keane's departure from Old Trafford in November 2005.*

‘ Roy Keane has been a fantastic servant for Manchester United. The best midfield player in the world of his generation, he is already one of the great figures in our club's illustrious history. **’**

Sir Alex *on Keano*

❛Anyone that witnessed what George could do on the pitch wished they could do the same. He made an immense contribution to the game, and enriched the lives of everyone that saw him play. It is a very sad day.❜

Sir Bobby Charlton *marks the passing of George Best in November 2005.*

' I'm very proud to have scored 100 goals for United. **'**

Ruud Van Nistelrooy *reaches his ton at Everton in February 2004, after just 131 games.*

❝ His whole meaning of life is about Manchester United. **❞**

Sir Alex *on captain Gary Neville.*

‘ After Philip left, I had half an
hour to myself driving in my car
and I did think: 'This isn't going
to last forever. I'd better
enjoy this.' ’

Gary Neville *on life at Old Trafford after brother*
Phil joined Everton in the summer of 2005.

❝ Before I came here, the fans probably thought: 'Alan Smith... mouthy so-and-so!' But when you're out there fighting for them, their perceptions change and they see a different side of you! ❞

Alan Smith

‘ You always set out at the start
of the season at this club to try
and win a trophy, and we've
done that. I'm very pleased for
the players and for the fans. ’

Sir Alex *on the 2004 FA Cup triumph.*

❛I never celebrate goals. Everyone else goes up and I stay with the goalkeeper. I've always done it.❜

Gabriel Heinze

❝ I hope fans will mention my name like they mention Peter Schmeichel's. **❞**

Edwin van der Sar

'I have been here since I was
a young boy and I have grown
very fond of the club and the fans,
they have been an integral part
of my life.'

Ryan Giggs

‘ To think Ryan joined as a 13-year-old boy – and to be at a club for 20 years is unique in this era. ’

Fergie *praises Giggs as the Welshman commits to United until June 2008.*

'Football, eh! Bloody hell!'

Sir Alex Ferguson
*in the tunnel minutes after United's last-gasp
European Champions League Final
win in May 1999*